TO CR ~~EATIVE POWER~~

UNLOCK
YOUR CREATIVE
GENIUS !

By

Ron Dalrymple, Ph.D.

Second Edition
(c) Copyright 2016, Dr. Ron Dalrymple

Celestial Gifts Publishing
POB 4466, N. Ft. Myers, FL 33918

8 DAYS TO CREATIVE POWER
Unlock Your Creative Genius !

Formerly:
INCREASE YOUR POWER OF CREATIVE THINKING IN EIGHT DAYS

Ron Dalrymple, Ph.D.
Second Edition

Published by:
Celestial Gifts Publishing
Post Office Box 4466
N. Ft. Myers, FL 33918 U.S.A.
drrondal@hotmail.com,
www.drrondalrymple.com

8 DAYS TO CREATIVE POWER
Unlock Your Creative Genius !

Includes bibliographical references.
((Topical Headings:
1.) Creativity.
2.) Imagination.
3.) Creative arts. 4.) Manifestation.
5.) Inventions. 6.) Awakening.
7.) Innovation. 8.) Creative genius.

First Edition, 1985
© Copyright 1985 Dr Ron Dalrymple
ISBN 0-912957-41-6
Library of Congress Catalog No.:
85-50428

Second Edition, 2016
(c) Copyright 2016 Dr. Ron Dalrymple
ISBN-13: 978-1539059530
ISBN-10: 1539059537

Publisher's Cataloging-In-Publication Data (Prepared by The Donohue Group, Inc.)

Names: Dalrymple, Ron.
Title: 8 days to creative power : unlock your creative genius! / by Ron Dalrymple, Ph.D.
Other Titles: Eight days to creative power

Description: Second edition. | Ft. Myers, FL : Celestial Gifts Publishing, [2016] | First edition published as: Increase your power of creative thinking in eight days! San Jose,

Calif. : Supreme Grand Lodge of
AMORC, ©1985. | Includes
bibliographical references.
Identifiers: ISBN 978-1-5390-5953-0 |
ISBN 1-5390-5953-7
Subjects: LCSH: Creative thinking —
Problems, exercises, etc. | Creative
ability--Problems, exercises, etc. |
Imagination--Problems, exercises, etc.
Classification: LCC BF408 .D35 2016 |
DDC 153.3/5--dc23

WARNING - DISCLAIMER

This book is designed to provide information and creative ideas relative to the subject matter covered. It is sold with the understanding that the publisher and author are not engaged in rendering professional psychological services or consulting services of any kind. If professional psychological or other services are required, a competent professional should be sought.

It is not the purpose of this book to reprint or represent all the information or ideas pertaining to this subject matter, but rather complement, amplify and supplement other texts. For more information see References or consult other sources.

This book can be used as a source of stimulation and insight, but not as the ultimate resource on psychological procedures, concepts or issues. Other resources will present radically different views, and this work is in no way intended to usurp or contradict those divergent points of view.

The purpose of this book is to educate and entertain. The author and publisher shall have neither liability nor responsibility to any person or entity with respect to any loss or damage caused or alleged to be caused directly or indirectly by the informatIon and ideas contained in this book.

WARNING - DISCLAIMER.

ABOUT THE AUTHOR

Dr. Ron Dalrymple has been a licensed psychologist in Maryland, Pennsylvania, Missouri, Kansas, Arkansas, Colorado, Idaho, Florida, Arizona and New Zealand, with a special interest in the higher, seldom understood powers of the mind. He received his Ph.D. in psychology from the University of Maryland in 1984.

Combining years of clinical experience with research in physics, topological mathematics and philosophical analyses of Eastern and Western origins, he devised a meta-theoretical system of thought now expressed as Quantum Field Psychology.

He is a member of Mensa, is a Diplomate in Forensic Psychology, belongs to numerous psychological associations and is listed in Who's Who in America, Who's Who in Editors, Writers and Poets, Who's Who in the East, Who's Who in the World, and Who's Who in U.S. Authors and Writers.

He wrote a newspaper column for five years titled "The Voice Within," and did a radio talk show in Maryland by the same title.

His motivational books include **The Inner Manager**, **Increase Your Power of Creative Thinking in Eight Days**, **I Love You, God**, and **Quantum Field Psychology**, listed elsewhere in this publication, all best-sellers.

He produced a best-selling film about the discovery of Quantum Field Psychology, **Paradise Found 2015**.

All of his works are found on Amazon.com.

ACKNOWLEDGEMENTS

The author would like to give special thanks to Dr. Bruce Fretz at the University of Maryland in College Park, Maryland, who helped encourage and guide the doctoral dissertation research that led to the development of this book.

His ability to help differentiate creativity approaches and integrate them into a systematic program to stimulate and assess adult creativity was a significant contribution to this work.

Thanks also to the many students who participated in creativity development classes given over the years by the author.

FOREWORD

The purpose of this book is to help the reader think creatively throughout the day, developing creative thinking patterns, a creative self-image and creative habits a continuous part of life.

One of the greatest difficulties in transforming oneself into a more creative person is found in working through the negative emotions and beliefs we have long internalized, many of which are reinforced by negative attitudes and interactions with others.

Negative beliefs and emotions become lodged in the subconscious mind, and drive the system automatically until they are consciously changed. This takes considerable effort and persistence, since the deeply embedded negative emotions tend to link to many different thoughts, attitudes and other feelings.

Many of these beliefs and behaviors are dysfunctional, producing a continuing litany of interactions and relationships that enmesh the person in a constellation of confusion.

A virtual labyrinth of interconnected thoughts, emotions and behaviors have to be transformed, one-by-one, until they are all resolved.

This book was created to help the reader achieve that goal. The intent is for the reader to use these creative thinking patterns, attitudes and emotions throughout the day, until they become internalized in the subconscious mind and begin to drive the system.

Creative thinking affirmations should be repeated many times throughout the day, and memorized for future use. As you practice these, your own creative affirmations, attitudes and behaviors will occur to you.

Use them all with persistence, allowing the deeper mysteries of mind to manifest in your life.

—- Dr. Ron Dalrymple, September 16, 2016.

CONTENTS

Introduction 17

First Day: Initial Self-Assessment 23

Second Day: Developing a 40
Creative Self-Attitude, Part 1

Third Day: Developing a 67
Creative Self-Attitude, Part 2

Fourth Day: Practicing Creativity 98
Part 1

Fifth Day: Thinking in Creative 109
Patterns, Part 1

Sixth Day: Thinking in Creative 144
Patterns, Part 2

Seventh Day: Practicing Creativity 180
Part 2

Eighth Day: Final Self-Assessment 190

Calculating Your Creativity Quotient 207

Conclusion 213

References 217

Other Books by Dr. Ron Dalrymple 229

INTRODUCTION

This book is about creativity and you.

Creativity is the ability to bring new or unique things into being. It is the basis of invention, writing, art, music, mathematics, philosophy, thought, and life itself.

It is the source of humor and the wellspring of health and happiness. It can be applied to any and all aspects of our lives, in order to broaden and bring depth to our daily realities.

Everybody is creative in different ways, but we are often not fully aware of it. We each possess a vast reservoir of creative potential, just waiting to be released.

To release this potential, all we need do is learn what creativity is and how to apply it to our own lives. Once we learn how to do this, we are each capable of amazing things.

The purpose of this book is to help you develop your creative potential in three different ways. First, you will be shown how to change your attitudes about yourself and your creative potential.

Many people are astonished to learn that by simply thinking about themselves in creative ways, their minds begin to function more creatively.

A number of techniques and examples will be given showing you how to achieve this.

The second way in which this book helps you develop your creative potential is by showing you a number of patterns of thinking that are readily applied to creative endeavors.

These simple and easy-to-apply techniques allow you to approach a wide range of problems with a new and flexible repertoire of thinking and problem-solving skills.

The third way this book helps develop your creative potential is by giving you a lot of practice in performing creative tasks. You will have the opportunity to complete a wide range of creative endeavors.

You will have the opportunity to complete a wide range of creative exercises, in order to practice the newly creative attitudes and thinking patterns you will be learning.

The material in this book is divided into an eight-day program. The first and eighth days allow you to assess the levels of your creative functioning before and after you complete the creativity program contained in the book.

In this manner, you will be able to see how much you have learned and how your creative abilities have grown.

The second and third days of the program teach you how to improve your creative self-concept, by showing you how to stop thinking negatively about yourself, and to replace any negative thoughts and feelings with positive ones.

Three different approaches are given for you to accomplish this. The fourth day gives you a number of creativity experiences to complete, which simulate a wide range of mental processes.

By combining the positive thinking of the second and third days with the practice exercises of the fourth day, you are given a chance to put the positive thinking to work.

The fifth and sixth days teach you a number of specific thinking patterns and techniques that can be applied to many different types of problems and situations which demand creative solutions.

You will learn how to analyze problems by stretching your imagination and by rearranging your thoughts at will, discovering in the process that your creative power is only limited by your self-doubts and by whatever habits of rigid thinking you presently maintain.

The seventh day again allows you to practice using your expanding creative abilities in a number of different and interesting ways.

It gives you a chance to use your newly acquired creative thinking patterns and your new creative self-attitude in tackling exercises.

Once you have learned to use these techniques in a diversity of ways, you should be able to apply them to better your daily life.

As previously mentioned, the eighth day allows you to reassess your creative abilities after completing the creativity program.

You will be able to determine how much progress you've made already, and you should have many ideas and insights about your own creative processes to take with you.

Ideally, you will have learned to think about yourself in a more creative manner, and you will know how to apply your creative abilities to many different problems and opportunities.

Just relax and enjoy yourself.

FIRST DAY

First Day: Initial Self-Assessment

The following three exercises allow you to determine, or measure, your present level of creative ability in terms of using your imagination and your reasoning power.

Each exercise is termed a measure and is self-explanatory. It provides you with a suggested time limit for completing the measure.

To score each measure, simply add up the number of answers you gave within the suggested time limit.

These scores will later be compared with the test scores you obtain after completing the creativity program.

The first measure determines your ability to make up ideas at will which describe a given phrase or expression.

This gives you a chance to let your imagination play, to dream up anything you want that fits the given phrase. The goal is to think of as many things as you can within the given time limit.

The second measure determines your ability to think of as many associations as you can which fit a given category. As you progress through the measure, the categories of association become more and more complex, challenging you to really concentrate.

As with the first measure, the goal is to think of as many things as you can within the given time limit.

The third measure assesses your ability to think in terms of relationships. You will be asked to think of answers that have different types of relationships to the given words.

As with the other measures, the goal is to think of as many answers as you can within the given time limit.

If you have difficulty with any of these measures, don't worry about that! The entire purpose of this book is to show you how you can improve your creative abilities, with the hope that everyone can learn something from the creativity program that follows.

It is important to remember that creativity is a set of skills, which can be learned by virtually everyone. All it takes is a little time and energy.

Once you have learned to expand your creative abilities, you will be able to apply them in a multitude of ways in your daily life.

It is essential to realize that by using the power of creative thinking we are able to change and improve the troubled world we live in. So relax, enjoy yourself, and learn all you can.

The future is in our hands.

When you are ready, please proceed to the next page and begin the first day of the creativity program.

Measure 1

In this measure, you will be asked to think of as many words or phrases as you can which can be used to describe the given phrase.

For example, if you were asked to respond to the expression "*The man was as tall as* ," you might answer with many different words and phrases. Some of these might be "*the trees,*" "*the sky,*" "*Wilt Chamberlain,*" and so on.

Your goal here is to think of as many answers to the given phrases as you can. Your score on this measure will be the number of words and phrases you write down which somehow describe the given phrases.

It is important to time yourself on this measure so that this beginning score can later be compared to your final score on an equivalent measure. Allow yourself exactly *five minutes* to compare this measure.

When you are ready, begin on the next page, and be sure to allow yourself exactly *five minutes* working time.

In a separate notebook, write as many words and phrases as you can, which complete the given phrases below:

The mountain air smelled like:

The candy tasted like:

The ocean looked like:

The touch of the sun was as warm as:

After you have completed Measure 1 within the five-minute time limit, simply add up the number of separate words and phrases you wrote down for all four parts of the measure combined.

For example, if you gave five answers to each of the first two questions, and seven answers to each of the third and fourth questions, your total score for the measure would be 24.

Write your total score in your separate notebook.

Measure 1 Total Score:

Measure 2

In this measure, you will be given certain words or combinations of words, and your task will be to list as many associations to the words as you can.

For example, if you were asked, *"Name everything you can that is orange,"* you might answer with *"the sun,"* *"a beach umbrella,"* *"oranges from Florida,"* and so on.

As with the first measure your goal is to think of as many answers to the given words as you can.

Your score on this measure will be the number of things you write down which fit the category described by the given words.

It is important to time yourself on this measure so your score can be compared to the equivalent measure given at the end of the creativity program.

Allow yourself exactly *two minutes* to complete each of the three parts of this measure (*6 minutes total* time).

When you are ready, turn to the next page and begin.

In your notebook, write down as many things as you can think of, which fit the given categories below:

Name everything you can that is blue:

Name everything you can that is blue and round:

Name everything you can that is blue, round and cold:

After you have completed Measure 2 within the six-minute time limit, simply add up the number of separate things you wrote down for all three parts of the measure combined.

Write your total score in your notebook.

Measure 2 Total Score:

Measure 3

In this measure, you will be given a certain word, and your task is to think of as many answers as you can that have different relationships to that word.

You will be asked to think of synonyms, antonyms, and words that rhyme with the given word.

For example, if you were given the word *tight*, you would be asked to list as many words as you can that rhyme with tight.

Next, write as many words as you can that have the same meaning as tight; then as many words as you can that have the opposite meaning from tight.

Your score on this measure will be the number of answers you write down which properly relate to the given word.

As with the previous two measures, it is important to time yourself so your score can be compared to the equivalent measure given at the end of the creativity program.

Allow yourself exactly *two minutes* to complete each of the three parts of this measure (6 *minutes total* time).

When you are ready, proceed to the next page and begin.

The given word is *cold*, as in "not hot."

Write in your notebook as many words as you can that rhyme with or sound like cold:

Write in your notebook as many words as you can that have the same or similar meaning to the word cold:

Write in your notebook as many words as you can that have the opposite or nearly opposite meaning to the word cold:

After you have completed Measure 3 within the six-minute total time limit, simply add up the number of separate things you wrote for all three parts of the measure.

Write your total score in your notebook.

Measure 3 Total Score:

SECOND DAY

Second Day:
Developing a Creative Self-Attitude

Part 1

Today gives you the chance to see how you think about yourself, in terms of your creative abilities and potential. You will learn how your present attitudes were formed and how those attitudes can be changed at will.

When these attitude-changing techniques are applied to creativity, you can learn to become more creative by thinking more creatively about yourself and about your ability to handle any number and range of problems.

The third day of the program, which is "Developing a Creative Self-Attitude, Part 2," continues with these techniques.

Relax, and get ready to think differently about yourself!

When you are ready, turn to the next page and begin.

Developing a Creative Self-Attitude

Part 1

The purpose of this discussion is to help you understand how people form attitudes about creativity, how these attitudes affect one's creative abilities, and how these attitudes can be changed at will.

First, we will consider your previous creative activities, how you became involved in them, and the types of experiences which might have interfered with your creative potential.

Second, we will examine a general procedure for changing how you think about both your creative potential and your approaches to being creative.

Finally, we will present three ways in which you can apply this procedure toward your creative development.

Current Attitudes

Creativity is generally defined as being the tendency or ability to produce unusual or original responses to a given situation or set of stimuli.

Most people are potentially creative in many ways but may not be fully aware of it.

Learning how to think about ourselves differently can help expand our creative abilities, so we can learn to generate original ideas and productions in a multitude of areas.

Before preceding to a discussion of how to change the attitudes we have about creativity and creative endeavors, it is first helpful to understand our present attitudes, how we formed them and how they affect us.

Exercise 1: In your notebook, list what you consider to be three of your major or favorite accomplishments of a creative nature. Include everything that you feel is creative, whether you think others would agree or not.

For example, you might list drawings or paintings you've done, poems or stories you've written, things you've built, or unusual thoughts you've had.

1)

2)

3)

The types of creative activities we enjoy usually develop because we seem to have some talent in those endeavors, or we are exposed to activities through other people or through some form of training.

Often we work hard at developing the things we already seem to be good at doing. In this manner, it is easy to overlook other areas of creativity which we might otherwise develop.

This tendency is unfortunate since the same principles of expanding our creative potential apply regardless of the specific areas involved.

Once the principles are learned, they can be applied to any project or activity.

Understanding how we developed our present abilities is therefore important to learning how to generalize and expand beyond them.

Exercise 2: Take a moment to think about each of the answers you gave in Exercise 1, considering how you acquired or developed those creative accomplishments.

Then, in the space provided on the next page, briefly describe the most important experiences or influences which helped you produce those achievements.

You might list parents, teachers, or friends who helped you develop specific abilities, or you might have read certain books which influenced you.

For example, you might list that a certain teacher taught you to write creative fiction or that a friend taught you how to paint.

It is also important to understand which influences and experiences have impeded or interfered with our creative development.

Sometimes our creative attempts are not met with approval from others, or we might have experienced other frustrations when undertaking various creative endeavors.

These types of experiences might make us believe we lack creative potential, thereafter diverting our interests from creative projects. In order to unravel these negative influences, we must first be aware of where and how they occur.

Exercise 3: In your notebook, list the experiences you've had which have interfered with your creative activities.

Following this list, write the creative things you might have accomplished by now, were it not for these negative influences.

For example, you might list specific experiences when some one discouraged your creative efforts, and the things you might have accomplished otherwise.

Over the past several decades, much research has shown that creativity is often discouraged in our school systems.

We are taught from an early age to behave in certain ways, to conform to the expectations of others, and not to deviate very far from those expectations.

If we do deviate from the established norms, we are chastised and ridiculed by others.

Since creativity involves the production of unusual responses or ideas, these types of activities are in complete opposition to the conformist norms set by our peers and our social systems.

These negative circumstances can destroy our creative endeavors or distort them in some manner. These effects can further degrade our self-concept about our creative potential.

Other forms of negative self-statements also influence our creative self-concept. Self-statements are the internal monologues about ourselves.

When we develop many negative self-statements as a result of life's experiences, these greatly limit our creative potential.

Part of becoming more creative involves learning how to stop referring to ourselves in negative ways, and replacing the negative self-statements with positive ones.

This simply entails breaking old habits and replacing them with new ones. The first step in this process is to be aware of the many ways in which we think negatively about ourselves.

Exercise 4: List below all the ways you think negatively about yourself. For example, you might list the ideas that you can't write well, you're poor at mathematics, and you're not as popular as you would like to be.

Thinking for a moment about these negative self-statements, how might these interfere with your creative potential?

For example, if you would like to learn how to play the piano, but you have maintained for years the self-perception that you are all thumbs, how would this influence your rate of growth as a pianist?

It could slow you down at the least, possibly until you either quit piano or learned to change your self-perception.

The material that follows presents a number of ways in which you can learn to change how you think about yourself, both as a creative individual and in more general terms.

A number of different approaches will be presented which are designed to accomplish this.

Remember:

Most people are potentially creative in many ways but may not be fully aware of it. Some of life's experiences encourage our creative endeavors, and other experiences interfere.

These experiences help shape our self-concepts, which then greatly influence our continuing interests in creative activities.

Internal self-statements reinforce and maintain our self-concepts, and these self-statements can be changed at will.

Changing Attitudes

Creativity, rather than being identified with any specific product, involves different patterns of thinking, feeling and behaving. These patterns intimately involve the self- concept.

As discussed in the previous section, the self-concept is reinforced and maintained by the self-statements with which we address ourselves.

If we think of ourselves in a negative manner, then we tend to create negative experiences in our lives, and we hamper our creative potential.

Conversely, if we learn to think of ourselves in a positive manner, then we tend to create more positive experiences in our lives, and we facilitate our creative abilities in general. By regulating our self-statements, we shape our self-concept.

Learning to change how we think about ourselves can seem difficult at first, because of the persistence of our present habits. As we gradually effect the change and construct a more positive self-concept, this, too, becomes persistent and resistant to change.

Replacing our negative self-statements with positive ones is executed with a simple procedure. This first step is to be aware of our negative self-statements, as was outlined in Exercise 4.

Briefly glance through the answers you gave to that exercise. These self-statements will now serve as cues when you are thinking negatively about yourself.

Whenever you realize that you are repeating one of these internal self-statements, or you find yourself thinking negatively about yourself in any manner, tell yourself to stop!

This is most important, so please repeat this idea to yourself several times. Whenever you find yourself repeating an internal monologue of a negative nature, or realize you are thinking negatively about yourself or others in any way, tell yourself to stop!

This must be done forcefully, since habitual self-statements tend to work in an automatic manner, often escaping our conscious awareness.

We must begin now to exert a stronger influence over these processes in order to change them.

Once the negative self-statements are interrupted in this manner, they can be replaced with positive self-statements, which we will develop in this program.

Then, each time you stop a negative thought, you will repeat a positive self-statement five times to yourself, to help establish it as a new habit.

This must be done every time you become aware of a negative self-statement, which requires some small degree of diligence at first.

This is because habits formed long ago tend to pop up in unexpected ways and at unexpected times.

The process becomes easier with time, and then virtually automatic. Your negative self-statements become replaced with positive ones.

There are a number of types of positive self-statements that can be used in this procedure. After discussing each of the three basic forms of statements, we will work at developing some self-statements of our own.

The first form of positive self-statement that we will consider is based upon attitudinal and personality factors.

These are statements designed to help us see ourselves and think about ourselves as unique, creative individuals, capable of doing many things beyond our present limits of self-perception.

It is important for each of us to realize that we are indeed individuals, and either possess now or can develop a number of undiscovered talents.

Equally important is the realization that each of us must discover for ourselves what these talents are, and how we might best apply them to our lives.

We cannot rely on parents, peers, or anyone else to tell us what to do or who to be. We can learn much from others, but the decisions we make in life have to be our own, since we are the ones who must live with the consequences.

Samuel Johnson reflected this idea with, *"No one ever yet became great by imitation."*

This concept was echoed by W. Somerset Maugham with, *"Impropriety is the soul of the wit."*

Each of these thinkers was expressing the idea that creativity and individuality go hand in hand.

Learning to relax and be oneself allows the boundaries of the mind to expand and embrace more unusual ideas, things which might not occur to other individuals.

Being creative includes understanding there are often no right or wrong answers, and the opinions of other people are sometimes perfectly irrelevant.

However, when we step aside from the prevailing paths of conformity in this world, we are likely to encounter some degree of rejection and scorn from others.

Peer pressure and most social institutions work to reinforce conformism and to punish any deviation from the established norms.

Individuals often seek to control one another for personal reasons, which greatly impedes creative productivity.

Jonathan Swift rather cynically said, *"When a true genius appears in this world, you may know him [or her] by this sign, that the dunces are all in the confederacy against him [or her]."*

Learning to be unique and individualistic involves some degree of risk-taking. This includes establishing our own set of values, rather than turning to others for continuous reinforcement or support.

Fortunately, becoming more creative tends to increase our self-confidence, just as developing our self-confidence tends to increase our creative activities. Self-confidence furthers our abilities to take risks and to set our own values.

As we reconstruct how we think about ourselves and how we allow others to influence us, we are creating the proper conditions for our creative ideas to emerge.

Psychologists Rogers and Maslow each emphasize the importance of establishing an environment of psychological safety and freedom, within which creativity will flourish naturally.

Summarizing the above concepts, creativity is facilitated by:

(1) Thinking about ourselves as unique individuals.

(2) Realizing we are each capable of finding our own answers to life's problems.

(3) Understanding we do not need to bow to peer or social pressures in most cases.

(4) Realize that risk-taking and self-confidence are important characteristics to develop.

A list of self-statements based on these and related ideas follows.

I will be creative, unique.

I can find my own answers to problems.

I am not afraid to take risks of a reasonable nature.

I have every reason to believe in myself.

I will not worry about what others think.

Most questions are not a matter of right and wrong.

I will not think of myself or others negatively.

I will relax and be myself.

Exercise 5: Read through the above list of statements several times and choose the two or more you like the best, or which make the most sense to you.

In your notebook, write down the statements you have chosen.

Following this, allow your mind to wander for a moment, and see what other positive self-statements come to mind. Write these down as well.

Read through your list of self-statements several times, and tell yourself you will remember them. From now on, whenever you find yourself thinking negatively about yourself, tell yourself to stop!

Replace the negative self-statement with positive ones that fit the situation.

Take a moment to repeat your positive self-statements several times, saying each one at least five times.

Make a habit of repeating these statements to yourself every night before you go to bed, and when you wake up in the morning.

This concludes the second day of the creativity program. Remember everything you have learned today, for you will find innumerable ways to apply these techniques in your daily life.

THIRD DAY

Third Day:
Developing a Creative Self-Attitude

Part 2

Today continues with the techniques designed to help you think about yourself in a creative manner.

Changing our habits and self-attitude takes time, especially because the old habits and attitudes can be resistant to change, often popping up when we least expect them.

In order to counteract and change unwanted habits, we must be persistent in our efforts to remove them. This requires being aware of our thinking processes as they occur.

We begin this procedure by telling ourselves to be more aware of our thoughts and feelings as they arise, so we can stop the negative thoughts and feelings and replace them with positive ones.

Do not be discouraged if this method seems difficult to perform at first, practice makes it easier.   It becomes a habit.

Take a moment to review the positive self-statements you learned yesterday, and decide to make them a part of your life.

Relax, and enjoy the thrill of gaining more control over your life! When you are ready, turn the page and begin.

Developing a Creative Self-Attitude

Part 2

The second form of positive self-statement we will discuss is based on allowing the conscious mind to relax its usual boundaries.

A tsunami of creativity flows from connecting the conscious mind to the unconscious...and even the superconscious mind.

The well-known process of free association is based on the concept of this interaction, where one relaxes the usual ego, or conscious controls, and states whatever comes to mind.

Free association is executed when one is relaxed, without muscular exertion or sensory distraction, and simply speaks as if involved in a rambling conversation.

The loosening of the usual conscious controls allows forgotten memories and unwanted relationships to surface, a process that helps the individual gain self-insight and understanding, especially when guided by a trained therapist.

Similarly, a variation of free association can be used when searching for creative ideas.

Here, we do not totally allow our thoughts to ramble, but rather allow them to vacillate around a given idea or subject.

For example, if we wish to think of new and unusual uses for a piece of string, we allow our thoughts to fluctuate around the idea of the string.

In this sense, our thoughts are centered on a specific point of reference, as opposed to Freudian free association, where our thoughts are not specifically centered.

This application of free association to creativity might better be termed *relaxed attention*, since we are lowering the usual boundaries of the ego while maintaining some degree of attention as to where our thoughts are leading.

The important similarity between these two forms of free association is that each taps into unconscious and preconscious material, giving the conscious mind a greater field of vision.

Relaxed attention involves some degree of detachment from our thoughts, where we observe the thoughts passing through the mind like an impartial bystander.

This degree of detachment allows the processes of the mind a wide range of movement, and avails the individual a means of observing and absorbing the processes that occur.

This technique is an effective means of balancing control with the loosening of control over the conscious processes.

Too much control leads to rigidity and little creativity, and too little control produces a lack of awareness as to where the thoughts are progressing.

Finding our individual sense of balance between control and the slackening of control requires some experimentation and practice.

One approach to finding our balance is to sit or lie down in a relaxed position and observe our thoughts as if we were watching a mental television screen.

This process is facilitated by closing our eyes and imagining a blank white screen stretched across the inside of the forehead, across which the images and thoughts will progress.

Take a moment to close your eyes, imagine such a screen, and observe whatever appears there. Do this before proceeding.

This process of imagining a screen involves the faculty of *visualization*, since the images and thoughts occur in a visual sense.

Free association was originally developed as a semantic process, but relaxed attention can be approached from either the verbal or visual modes.

That is, we can practice observing verbal and visual streams of consciousness when engaging in creative endeavors.

The entire purpose of these procedures is to find creative ideas or answers to problems by tapping the subconscious mind, which can lead to accessing the superconscious mind.

The superconscious mind is here presented as the very core of our being, and the essence of who we are.

More on this is presented in **The Inner Manager** (2016), and **Quantum Field Psychology** (2016).

Other theorists present similar concepts, such as the idea of *regression in service of the ego,* where we voluntarily relax ego control in order to "regress" to more primitive levels of thought.

Another group of theorists conceives of creativity as controlled regression, to passively experience fantasy and primitive levels of thought, which are then integrated with reality.

This latter group of investigators has also used hypnosis as a means of tapping the subconscious, or perhaps superconscious minds.

Self-suggestion is a means of applying a form of self-hypnosis to our creative endeavors. Self-suggestion simply involves "feeding" or programming the subconscious mind to do what we desire.

This approach can open access to the superconscious mind.

We tell the subconscious mind a number of times what to do, then temporarily put it aside, assuming in the process the job will be accomplished.

By forgetting about the process after giving the subconscious its instructions, we are sending a message into that region and then allowing the subconscious to take over the process.

This is an important point, since consciously continuing to think the original directive will simply keep the thought in the conscious mind, preventing the subconscious from doing the creative work.

The self-statements we are developing are a specific form of self-suggestion.

Self-suggestions can be more complex, such as a writer directing the subconscious to formulate a plot for a new novel.
Or a mathematician asking the subconscious for help in solving a theorem.

It is important to forget about the process, once the subconscious is told what to do, while we wait for an answer.

The subconscious mind will project ideas and insights into the conscious mind when it is ready to do so, and this can happen at any time.

Characteristically, it happens when we least expect it. The best way we can prepare for it is simply to be open to it and wait for it to come.

Should we keep thinking the original directive on a conscious level, repeating it endlessly to ourselves, we will only interfere with the process.

This indicates an essential aspect of properly using the self-statements we are developing.

Once the statements have been repeated to oneself a number of times, they must be forgotten about for the time being, allowing the subconscious mind to go to work.

The appropriate statements are not thought about consciously again until the need arises.

That is, when we again realize we are thinking negatively about ourselves, then the positive self-statements are used again to replace the negative ones.

Summarizing the above concepts, before proceeding to our list of self-statements for this section, we know that creativity is facilitated by:

(1) Relaxing the usual boundaries between the conscious and subconscious minds, so original ideas and insights can surface from the subconscious into the conscious.

(2) *Relaxed attention,* a procedure similar to free association, where we observe the conscious processes like a detached bystander.

(3) Using a visual mental screen across which images and thoughts can progress.

(4) Using self-suggestions to feed directions to the subconscious mind. We then temporarily forget about the process and wait for the answers to come.

A list of self-statements based on these and related ideas follow:

I will release controls and let my mind wander.

I will use free association, and let ideas flow.

I will relax, and just let it happen.

I will let my ideas play.

I will feel like a bystander, observing my ideas flow through me.

I will let one answer lead to another.

I will observe my mental screen, allowing thoughts and images to flow across it.

I will use self-suggestion to program my subconscious mind, when searching for creative ideas, or to change how I think about things.

Exercise 6: As with the previous list of self-statements, read through the list above several times, and choose two or more which you like the best, or which seem to make the most sense to you.

In your notebook, write down the statements you have chosen. Following this, allow your mind to wander for a moment, and see what other positive self-statements come to mind. Write these down as well.

Read through this list several times, and tell yourself you will remember them. Whenever you find yourself thinking negatively about yourself, or want to generate creative ideas, tell yourself to **stop**!

Then feed your subconscious mind whichever self-statements seem appropriate to the situation. Take a moment to repeat the self-statements five times to yourself, before moving on to the next session.

This section is perhaps best concluded by John Locke, who reflected an idea similar to that of self-suggestion:

"The thoughts that come often unsought and, as it were, drop into the mind, are commonly the most valuable of any we have."

Exercise 7: Again repeat your list of self-statements, and then sit for a few moments in quiet relaxation to see what ideas come to mind. Write in your notebook whatever ideas occur to you.

The third and final form of positive self-statement is based on how we think about our mental capabilities.

A number of creativity researchers have focused on this approach, seeking to stimulate creative production by teaching individuals how to think differently about their problem-solving abilities.

William James expressed this idea with, *"Genius, in truth, means little more than the faculty of perceiving in an un-habitual way."*

Learning how to think positively about our problem-solving abilities requires some understanding of the problem-solving process.

Realizing that problems are a normal part of life, the first step is to anticipate we will be able to solve our problems as they arise.

This attitude greatly increases the likelihood that an adequate solution to the situation will be found.

Remaining optimistic about being able to solve our problems as they arise is not always easy.

One of the clearest identifying features of a problem is found within our emotional reaction to it.

Rather than becoming distracted by the emotion, we can use it as a cue to shift our attention to the problem that is causing the upset.

This is analogous to becoming aware of negative self-statements in order to replace them with positive ones.

Further, using the emotion as a cue to shift our attention, helps avoid making impulsive reactions to the problem.

Once we have recognized a problem exists and have focused our attention on it, we tell ourselves to gather more facts and information about it.

One technique useful here is known as *brainstorming*, a procedure similar to the previously discussed concepts of free association and relaxed attention.

The basic rules of brainstorming are:

(1) To rule out criticism.

(2) To allow any and all ideas to come to mind at first, no matter how improbable.

(3) Quantity of ideas will lead to more high quality ideas.

(4) Combining and improving upon ideas is encouraged, in a second phase of the brainstorming process.

When we try to generate alternative solutions to a problem, we   initially allow any and all ideas to come to mind, without attempting to evaluate them until later.

Separate ideas can be taken apart and recombined at will in the second, *critical process*, formulating whatever we wish.

Following the generation of as many alternative solutions as possible, we then move to that secondary, decision-making phase, so as to select the best strategy or strategies.

This requires making a prediction as to the likely consequences of each proposed choice or course of action.

We must also consider the relative ease of implementation of each course of action.

We then balance the possible effectiveness of the action against the expected difficulty of using it.

If none of the proposed alternatives seem feasible, then we return to the first phase, the generation of further alternatives.

Once a course of action is selected, we implement it and try it out. If the solution works, the problem is solved.

If the solution does not work, we might try other generated alternatives, returning to any phase of the procedure as required.

Summarizing the above concepts, before proceeding to our list of self-statements for this section, we know that finding creative solutions to problems is facilitated by:

(1) Learning to think for ourselves.

(2) Knowing we are capable of coping with and solving problems as they arise.

(3) Observing emotional reactions as cues, alerting us to the presence of a specific problem.

(4) Defining and formulating problems specifically.

(5) Generating and testing alternative solutions to problems.

A list of self-statements based on these and related ideas follow:

Every *"problem"* is only a challenge, and no challenge is a problem.

I can cope with any problems I encounter.

I can learn to perceive things in many different ways.

Problems are a normal part of life.

I will use emotional reactions as cues to the presence of problems.

I will not react impulsively to problems.

I will define every detail related to a problem.

I will generate alternative solutions to the problem, without initially judging them.

I will evaluate and verify the alternatives only after several have been generated.

I can turn a given disadvantage into an advantage.

Exercise 8: As with the previous two lists of self-statements, read through the list just given several times, and choose two or more which you like best, or which seem to make the most sense to you.

In your notebook, write down the statements you have chosen. Following this, allow your mind to wander for a moment, and see what other positive self-statements come to mind. Write these down as well.

Read through this list several times, and determine to remember the statements.

Whenever you find yourself thinking negatively about yourself or your ability to face and solve a given problem, tell yourself to **stop**!

Repeat several times out loud (if possible) whichever self-statements seem appropriate to the situation. Then repeat the statements five times to yourself.

This concludes the description of positive self-statements based on the three approaches: attitudinal and personality factors, tapping the subconscious mind, and use of mental abilities.

Read through each of the three lists of self-statements and think about how you would use them in different situations.

For example, if you had to think of a title for a story you have written, you would first stop all negative thoughts about yourself and your ability to think of a title.

You might then use one of the statements from the first list, such as, "*I am creative and unique,*" and, "*I never worry what others think.*"

As you write some of the attempted solutions, you might find they don't work.

You might repeat to yourself some of the statements from the second list, such as, "*I will release controls and let my mind wander,*" and, "*I will let my ideas play.*"

Should the answers still be slow in coming, you could try some of the statements from the third list.

Perhaps, "*I can perceive this problem in a different way.*" And, "*I need to define every detail of the problem first.*"

If you still have not arrived at a solution after trying to stimulate ideas with the self-statements, you could use self-suggestions to your subconscious, instructing it to find solutions for you.

Then, all you need do is wait, being certain to continue a positive internal monologue.

We cannot determine when answers might appear or how, and must be open to possible solutions in whatever form they might appear.

Exercise 9: Once more, repeat your self-statements. Now, write in your notebook as many things as you can think of that are: round, blue, and warm.

Remember:

You can learn to increase your creative abilities by changing your attitudes about your creative potential.

By replacing your negative self-statements with positive ones, and by feeding self-suggestions to your subconscious mind, you can reformulate your self-concept and your creative activities at will.

Some of the major concepts upon which our self-statements are based include that creativity can be facilitated by:

Thinking of ourselves as being uniquely creative, self-confident, independent, and capable of taking risks.

Relaxing the boundaries between the conscious and subconscious minds, and observing the thought images that pass across our mental screen with a detached perspective.

Telling ourselves to define and formulate problems as they arise, searching for creative solutions until one is found and verified.

Most important of all, remembering to replace our negative self-statements with positive ones.

Remember also to repeat these statements to yourself every night before going to bed, and when you awaken in the morning.

As these concepts become second nature to you, you will be amazed to discover the powerful effect they have on your thinking and creative abilities.

This concludes the third day of the creativity program. Sleep well on these ideas, for tomorrow you will have a chance to put these techniques to work.

FOURTH DAY

Fourth Day: Practicing Creativity

Part 1

Today gives you a chance to put your evolving creative abilities to work. What follows are a number of different exercises.

Take a moment to look over the positive self-statements of the second and third days, and repeat them to yourself.

Focus on how the statements can be used when applied to solving a given problem, as outlined in the third day of the program.

You will now have a chance to directly apply this procedure to a number of different creativity tasks.

Remember to first stop all negative thoughts about yourself and your developing creative abilities, and then apply whichever of the statements seem to fit the problem.

You can also use self-suggestion and feed the statements to your subconscious, giving the subconscious a chance to go to work for you.

This latter procedure usually requires more time to work, although it can provide ideas immediately.

The following exercises give you recommended time limits with which to work. Try to follow these limits as closely as possible, to obtain the maximum benefit from the practice.

The seventh day of the program will present "Practicing Creativity, Part 2."

Now relax, and let your creative ideas flow!

When you are ready, turn the page and begin.

Practicing Creativity

Part 1

Exercise 10: This is a measure to see how many things you can think of that are alike in some way. For example, if you were asked to list all the things you can think of that are violet, you might list *"violets – the flower,"* *"twilight,"* and so on.

You may use one word, several words, or a phrase to describe each thing. Allow yourself about *three minutes* to complete this exercise.

The category is *"square."* List all the things you can think of in your notebook that are square.

Exercise 11: When you are thinking creatively, it is often helpful to think in sequences of images and words that are somehow linked together.

To practice thinking in sequences, this measure requires you to think of words having meanings the same as or similar to a given word.

For example, if you were given the word long, you might write "lengthy," "extended," "tiresome," and so on.

Write down as many words as you can think of, allowing yourself about *five minutes* to complete the exercise.

In your notebook, write as many words as you can think of that have similar meanings to the given words:

Quick   Weak   Heavy

Exercise 12: When trying to find creative answers, you can often see things in a new light by rearranging how you categorize certain objects or ideas.

You can practice this type of mental flexibility by listing as many objects as you can which belong to any given class of objects.

In this exercise, your task will be to list as many objects as you can which belong to the given class.

For example, if you were given the class "*dog,*" you might list "*terrier,*" "*spaniel,*" "*collie,*" and so on. Allow yourself about *two minutes* to complete this exercise.

In your notebook, list as many things as you can that belong to the class "metal."

Exercise 13: Creative ideas often come from finding new uses for common objects. In this exercise, you are to list as many uses as you can for the given object.

For example, if you were asked to list all the uses you can for a piece of string, you might include *"picture hanger,"* *"teeth cleaner,"* *"toy hat strap,"* and so on.

Your answers can be realistic or completely imaginary. Allow yourself about *five minutes* to complete this exercise.

In your notebook, list as many uses as you can for a *"tin can."*

Exercise 14: Another important aspect of creativity is learning how to express complex ideas in a simple form. One means of practicing this is by creating titles for a given story plot.

In this exercise, you will be given a story plot and asked to write as many appropriate titles as you can which represent a plot. The titles can be realistic or imaginative, but they must have some clear relationship to the given plot.

For example, if you were given a plot about a convicted felon becoming the President of the United States, you might call it, *"From Parolee to President."*

Or perhaps, *"Jail to the Chief."* Allow yourself about *three minutes* to complete this exercise.

In your notebook, write as many appropriate titles as you can for the following plot:

A poor immigrant came to the United States over one hundred years ago, and wanted to get rich.

He tried many different occupations, and finally decided that selling illegal and contraband goods was the most profitable business there was.

He eventually began selling arms and munitions to both sides of any given conflict, but found that when the conflict ended, so did his business.

He then decided to buy newspaper companies and sell propaganda as well, to ensure that worldwide conflicts could be sustained and even started.

Years later, one of his descendants continued his work with another marketing scam— the Cold War.

Exercise 15: Creative thinking often involves the process of abstraction, where we use metaphors, similes, puns, and other constructions to get our ideas across to others.

Many of these verbal constructions compare one thing to another.

In this exercise, you will be given an incomplete sentence and asked to complete the sentence by comparing the first part of the sentence with as many different things as you can.

For example, if you were given the incomplete sentence, *"Want is   ,   "* you might complete it with *"Want is the mistress of invention,"* and *"Want is the burden of the poor,"* and so on.

You can complete the given sentence with a single word, a series of words or a phrase, but make sure that the answer somehow relates to the first part of the sentence. Allow yourself about *two minutes* to complete this exercise.

In your notebook, complete the following incomplete sentence with as many comparisons as you can:

"Reason is _____ ."

FIFTH DAY

Fifth Day: Thinking in Creative Patterns

Part 1

Today gives you a chance to think about how our thinking processes occur.

Usually we think in specific patterns of mental analysis or reaction, and many of these patterns become habits, in the same way that self-attitudes become habits.

Once these habits are formed, we simply practice them without thinking about it. In this sense, our habits occur on a subconscious, or automatic level.

Fortunately, we can learn to change these habit patterns, in a manner similar to how we learned to change our self-attitudes.

The first step is to become aware of our current thinking patterns. The next step is to replace any habits we desire with more creative habits.

Take a moment to review how we replaced negative self-attitudes with positive ones.

The most important part of this is to be aware of what we are thinking. Then we can replace negative thoughts and feelings with positive ones.

The operation involved in this process is one of replacement.

By contrast, the operations involved in changing our specific patterns of mental analysis are somewhat more complex.

These operations involve not only being aware of our thoughts as they occur, but a number of techniques used to transform our thoughts.

These techniques might appear to be slightly imposing at first, but they become easy and fun to use once you make them habits.

The techniques can be used in solving everyday problems, in cracking mathematical equations, in dreaming up imaginative ideas, in creative writing, and in countless other forms of abstract and creative thinking.

Take your time learning these techniques, and be sure to apply your newly creative self-attitude and self-statements as you absorb these concepts.

Just before you go to sleep, repeat the ideas you are learning several times, allowing your subconscious to digest the information in myriad ways.

The sixth day of the program presents "Thinking in Creative Patterns, Part 2."

Relax, and let your mind expand!

When you are ready, please proceed to the next page and begin.

Thinking in Creative Patterns

Part 1

The purpose of this discussion is to help you think about how people think.

Our goal is to help you discover what underlies thinking processes, how different types of thinking habits develop, and how you can change your thinking habits at will.

First, we will discuss the most important different types of thinking. Second, we will examine how these different types of thinking are linked together to form larger and larger arrangements.

Finally, we will present various ways you can rearrange these concepts, to form whatever new concepts you wish.

Types of Thinking

Thinking processes often deal with complex arrangements of images, such as shapes, sounds, and colors.

These images represent either external objects or events, the self, or other internal thought images or concepts.

We will divide simple types of thought processes into three categories, those being *figural*, *semantic*, and *symbolic*.

Figural thought forms consist of images, figures, or likenesses of people, places, things, or events, either perceived from the environment, recalled from memory, or created by the imagination.

These concepts occur in a visual sense, and can be as simple as basic figures, such as circles, triangles, or squares.

Or, they can be as complex as the configurations of a modern abstract painting, or similar images conceived by the most vivid imagination. Colors are included in this category.

Semantic thought forms consist of verbal information, both in spoken and written form.

Speech involves auditory processes. Written language includes figural imagery, which conveys spoken or auditory information.

Semantic forms begin with sounds that are spoken in various rhythms and frequencies, and are written as syllables.

The sounds and syllables are combined to form words, phrases, sentences, paragraphs, and so on.

Various rules of formulation, or syntax, are used to make these combinations, rules which vary from language to language and from culture to culture.

Symbolic thought forms consist of signs, characters, figures, letters, numbers, tokens, and combinations of any of these, where each symbolic form is used to represent something else.

As mentioned, figural and semantic thought forms are specific types of symbolic concepts.

Other types of symbolic concepts are mathematics, musical notation, chemical symbols, business and commercial symbols, meteorological symbols, symbols denoting electronics, and many more.

Simple thinking processes combine to form compound thinking processes, which more closely describe our daily mental activities.

That is, any given thought might involve figural, semantic, and other symbolic properties simultaneously.

Different types of associations and relationships are used to bind elements together into these networks of thought.

As we shall see, it is by rearranging the associations and relationships between separate thoughts that one is able to generate creative ideas at will.

Habit thinking processes are thoughts and thought sequences which occur frequently, either due to over-learning of the information, or to emotional intensity having become attached to the information.

The associations and relationships binding the separate thought elements together into habit processes are often rigid and largely invariant.

Thereby, habitual thought processes often obscure other perceptions competing for conscious attention, blinding the individual to various forms of new information or ideas.

Fortunately, habit processes can be changed at will, by being aware of their presence, understanding how they are formed, and learning how they are altered. It is toward this end that we will now build.

Remember:

Thinking processes are built around figural, semantic, and symbolic forms. These are often linked by associations and relationships into simple, compound or complex thinking processes.

Associations are linkages between thought elements or thought compounds which may not be based on a rule, regulation, principle, code, or other constructed relationship.

Associations can be brought about by a number of different means. Separate elements of thought are placed in contiguity (nearness or proximity) to one another, where the occurrence of one of the elements evokes the occurrence of the other element(s).

This association becomes a learned process, a habit. The initial strength of the habit formed depends on how many times the association is made, and on the emotional intensity evoked by the association.

For example, we might require many trials to learn a phone number associated with a particular individual, if we have little interest in that person. However, if another individual excites our interest, the number might be learned instantaneously.

The habit strength of the association can change over time, depending on how often the association continues to be reinforced, and on the varying degree of emotional intensity elicited by the association.

The phone number example depicts a desirable association we wish to make, but there are other associations or habits we might wish to change.

To change our habits of association, we must either change how often an association is reinforced, or the emotional quality of the association.

For example, suppose we have learned to associate the idea of a dog with the idea of being bitten by a dog, and that this association elicits an intense fear of dogs.

In order to change this fearful association, we practice thinking about dogs in new ways.

We can focus on developing new thoughts in relationship to dogs, such as, *"Dogs are faithful," "Dogs are fun," "Dogs are furry,"* and so on. Here, we add new associations to the original one.

These new associations are then practiced while we feel positive emotions about dogs.

Feeling positively while we think positively about dogs will more rapidly replace the initial fear and negative associations. With time, the initial feelings and thoughts become habits.

This is often accomplished best while in a state of deep relaxation.

In this fashion, habits which have long been taken for granted can be changed.

We can learn to alter thoughts and feelings which we once accepted as *"reality,"* discovering in the process the essence of creativity.

Creative ideas are often found by learning how to perceive and how to think and feel in new ways, rather then rigidly responding in habitual patterns.

To better understand how these habit patterns often control our thoughts, it is helpful to understand the three processes by which associations are formed.

The first process is *repeated association*, where separate elements occur together enough times that the association between the elements becomes learned.

The association can include any combination of elements from the three thought forms----figural, semantic, or symbolic.

As a simple example, we might associate the color red with the image of a friend if that friend often wears red clothing.

The second process by which elements can become associated is *sensory association*, which occurs when any of the senses of sight, sound, touch, smell, or taste arouse any thought forms of a figural, semantic, or symbolic nature.

An association can be learned between an elicited thought form and the specific sensory stimulation which causes it to be aroused.

Or an association can be learned between two or more thought forms aroused by the same specific sensory stimulation.

An instance of the first situation is found when we associate the sound of a typewriter with the idea of doing office work.

An instance of the second situation is found if we associate the sound of a typewriter with the idea of doing office work, and with the sound of a machine gun.

The three thought forms of figural, semantic, and symbolic information are aroused differently by the separate senses.

Figural processes are most readily aroused by the sense of sight, but are also aroused by the other senses.

For example, the smell of honey might elicit the figural image of a brier patch, if we once encountered a beehive in the vicinity of a brier patch.

In this instance, the images of bees and beehives have become linked to the sensation of the smell of honey and to the image of a brier patch through direct association.

As a result of this linkage, the smell of honey becomes directly linked to the image of the brier patch as well.

As is often the case with associations, if A is associated with B and B is associated with C, then A becomes associated with C. In this manner, long chains of *association sequences* are formed.

Semantic thought forms are most readily aroused through the sense of hearing, where we respond verbally to spoken language, and through the sense of vision, when viewing written language.

Other senses can elicit semantic thought forms, such as the sense of touch used in Braille, and the scent of springtime giving rise to poetic expression.

Semantic thought forms often involve a combination of informational forms, integrating sensory images with memory and other perceptual forms, creating various levels of symbolic meaning.

For example, the word beach conveys a verbal and a visual message, while stimulating memories of our experiences at the beach.

Figural and semantic impressions are sparked by sensory impressions, such as heat, the touch of sand or pebbles, and the smell of sea air.

A single word can stimulate long association sequences of images, words, impressions, other symbols, and feelings, demonstrating the depth of semantic thought forms.

In general, different symbolic thought forms or combinations are aroused by the different senses. In addition to the figural and semantic examples given, many other examples can be drawn.

Symbolic thought forms are, in fact, different means of expressing the dimension and nature of things and events perceived through the senses, as well as the relationships inferred between observed phenomena.

The third and final association process by which elements of thought can become associated is *emotional association*.

As with repeated and sensory associations, emotional associations can link together elements or compounds of elements from the figural, semantic, and symbolic thought forms, often binding together vast complexes of interconnected thoughts.

Since many separate thought elements are initially formed with emotional components, the arousal of any given emotion can stimulate a multitude of associated thoughts.

It is this process of emotional association that accounts for the level of habit strength of many thought processes, as previously discussed.

That is, by increasing or decreasing the intensity of emotion attached to specific thoughts, we can alter the frequency of occurrence of those thought processes.

This process is enhanced by using sensory association simultaneously, since the emotion attached to specific thoughts often arises as a function of how the things or events are perceived which produce the thoughts.

For example, if we perceive earthworms wiggling about in the mud, we might feel disgust. The more intense this emotion is, the more strongly will it become attached to the thought of earthworms.

If we have previously attached feelings of disgust to other thoughts, such as snakes and other reptiles, then an association sequence is formed between earthworms, snakes, and other reptiles.

The connecting factor linking together these separate thoughts is the feeling of disgust. After these connections are made, if we should become caught in traffic and feel disgusted about it, then these other thoughts might come to mind.

The greater the habit strength of these associations, the more rapidly and forcefully will they come to mind.

To break the associative power of these connections, we can practice feeling differently about these thoughts, and we can practice associating different thoughts with the original ones.

These ideas were presented earlier in this section when discussing the alteration of habit strength.

In addition to these techniques, we can use simultaneous sensory association, where we change how we perceive things.

For example, we could decide to think about earthworms as simply being biological constructions of matter and energy, and nothing more.

Once this change is effected, feelings of disgust become dissociated from the thought of earthworms, and the connections to snakes and other reptiles as well---unless we similarly change how those creatures are perceived.

Therefore, emotional associations linking together different thought processes can be changed in any of these ways:

(1) Emotions attached to thoughts can be changed.

(2) Other thoughts attached to the initial thoughts can be changed.

(3) How we perceive the initial thoughts can be changed. In all of these cases, specific emotions link together a number of different thoughts.

(4) Emotional associations can also occur when a specific thought becomes linked to more than one emotion.

For example, if we have recently had some negative experiences with a good friend, then thinking about the friend will arouse both positive and negative feelings.

(5) These conflicting emotions will then produce contradictory perceptions concerning the individual, such that two or more distinct and opposing association sequences develop.

Thinking about the friend can then spark either or both of the association sequences.

(6) The contradictory sequences will tend to modify and alter one another, as well as confuse the individual, until the conflicting emotions underlying the sequences are resolved.

This situation might better be termed *emotional dissociation*, where the opposing emotions tend to disrupt thought processes, rather than link them together.

Summarizing these ideas about associations will help to clarify how these concepts can be used when we are trying to generate creative ideas.

Associations are linkages between thought elements or compounds which may or may not be based upon a rule.

Information from figural, semantic, or symbolic thought forms are brought together by repeated, sensory, or emotional contiguity.

The linkage becomes a learned process, where the habit strength of the association is determined by how often the association is reinforced, and by the emotional intensity of the association.

The emotional intensity is affected by the sensory quality of the perceptions arousing the thought processes involved.

The form of thoughts aroused is also influenced by the sensory quality of incoming information.

It follows from this description that sensory information, emotional reactions to the sensory information, and thoughts linked together through the actions of theses processes are all part of a system.

Changing one part of the system changes other parts.

This constitutes what is known as a *tensor field* (Dalrymple, 2016, Quantum Field Psychology).

Linkages between separate thought elements or compounds can be changed by altering the emotions bonding the thoughts together, by changing which elements associate with other elements, and by changing how we perceive incoming sensory information.

Given these concepts, suppose we wish to implement these principles in generating creative ideas. One approach to this would be to apply each one of the previous concepts to the task at hand.

For example, suppose we wish to list everything we can think of that is *brown*. Here, the task is to list all the figures, words, symbols, and concepts we can, expressing the idea of brown.

The first step would be to list all the associations initially attached to the idea of brown, within each of the figural, semantic, and symbolic forms.

Within the semantic form, we might think of the many words connecting brown, such as autumn, muddy, and dark.

Within the symbolic form, we might think of the letter b, then the number 2, since it is the second letter in the alphabet, and so on.

The second step would be to list all associations initially attached to the idea of brown, to see what further responses are sparked.

Associating the sense of vision with the idea of brown might make us think about the eye and the iris of the eye, as well as various brown things perceived in the environment.

In this example, the response of "eye" was already generated under the figural form of repeated associations, demonstrating that the successive steps of this technique may or may not produce unique responses.

The entirety of the steps as a whole, however, should produce a number of unique responses to the task. Each of the other sense channels of sound, smell, taste, and touch are next applied to the idea of brown.

The third step is to associate different emotions with the idea of brown, to see what further associative sequences might be found.

We might apply the emotion of comfort to the task, sparking the idea of a circle of warmth bonding people together in a brown cabin. We alternately apply positive and negative emotions to the task.

The fourth and final step is to look for combinations of responses derived from the responses found with the first three steps.

For example, we might combine the idea of a sunset with the iris of the eye, and suddenly think about a reflection of the sun in our eyes.

If we had already found many responses under the first three steps, then many more responses can often be found when looking at combinations of the initial responses.

To be exhaustive when looking at these various combinations, we would have to compare every response with every other response, and with every other combination of responses.

Since this task becomes infinitely large when carried to the extreme, we might continue with it only as long as it continues to yield unique responses.

To assist this process of looking for unique associations, please refer to Table 1: Association Table.

Due to the large numbers of responses that this series of steps can generate, Table 1 may not be large enough to hold them.

It is presented as a schematic means of organizing your associations to the given task.

Exercise 16: Using Table 1 as a guide, generate as many associations as possible with any one of the following items:

Spiral

Green

Seed

Remember:

Associations link together information from figural, semantic, and symbolic forms, linkages affected by repeated, sensory, or emotional contiguity.

These linkages can be changed by altering the emotions bonding the thoughts together, by changing which elements associate with which other elements, and by changing how we perceive incoming sensory information.

Table 1 can be used as a guide to generating new associations with a given figure, word, symbol, or concept.

These associations can be used to construct more complex creative structures, which will be presented in the material of the Sixth Day of the program, "Thinking in Creative Patterns, Part 2."

Before you go to sleep tonight, take a moment to review the many concepts you have just learned. Tell yourself that since you are becoming more and more creative every day, these concepts will become second nature to you.

Tell your subconscious to absorb these ideas thoroughly, and when you awaken in the morning you will have a new understanding of them. Further, tell your subconscious that, as time goes by, these ideas will become your daily habits.

Then simply clear your mind and relax, resting assured that your subconscious mind will take care of everything else.

When you awaken in the morning, try to recall as many of the ideas as you can, and tell yourself again that you will remember them and apply them on a daily basis.

Table 1: Association Table

| | Form | | |
	Figural	Semantic	Symbolic
Column			
Combinations			
<u>Associations</u>			
Repeated:			
Sensory:			
Sight			
Sound			
Smell			
Taste			
Touch			
Emotional:			
Positive			
Negative			
Row Combinations			
Row X Column			
Combinations			

SIXTH DAY

Sixth Day: Thinking in Creative Patterns

Part 2

Today continues with the creative thinking patterns we began yesterday. Take several moments to review the different types of thinking, and the forms of associations which link the thought processes together.

Consider how these constructions affect your thinking processes, and how they bind together your patterns of perception and analysis.

Focus again upon the idea of changing your thinking patterns and making them more creative, similar to how we considered altering our self-statements and self-attitude.

Decide to become more and more aware of your thoughts and the many patterns as they occur.

Recall how these patterns can be changed by finding new associations to many given concepts or mental processes, using the Association Table (Fifth Day) as a guide.

Today we will expand upon these concepts in our discussion of relationships.

Close your eyes for a moment and tell yourself that you are going to learn everything you can today, and that this new knowledge will add to your understanding of yesterday's discussion.

Just relax and watch your thoughts change form. When you are ready, turn the page and begin.

Thinking in Creative Patterns

Part 2

Yesterday, we discussed different types of thinking processes and some of the ways in which these processes are linked together.

We considered figural, semantic, and symbolic forms, which are linked together by associations and relationships.

Associations are linkages between thinking processes, which may or may not be based on a rule or other constructed relationship.

Associations can be formed by repeated, sensory, or emotional contiguity, such that a habit is formed between the associated elements.

Compounds of associations begin to form, such that each mental element is associated with a multitude of other elements.

We can learn to change these associative networks either by: altering the emotions which bind thoughts together; by changing which elements associate with which other elements; or by changing how we perceive incoming sensory information.

Table 1 was presented as a means of assigning the generation of new associations with a given figure, word, symbol, or concept.

The flexible generation of new associations can then be used in the construction of new relationships between elements, which is the topic of discussion today.

Relationships

Relationships are linkages between thought elements or compounds which are based upon a rule, principle, or other constructed process.

This is an important distinction, since associations are usually formed either by repetition or by sensory or emotional contiguity.

Relationships are intentionally formed by following some principle or set of principles, often creating a new element or product.

Relationships constitute much of our daily thinking, in addition to associations.

The elements or compounds linked together by relationships can be any of the processes drawn from the figural, semantic, or symbolic thought forms.

The relationships used to link these elements or compounds together are different for each type of symbolic expression used.

For example, in the figural domain, the relationship between two straight lines which intersect can be expressed by the angle between them.

The words oblique, acute, and perpendicular convey three very different relationships. In the semantic domain, nouns and verbs are related in that nouns represent people, places, things, or qualities.

As another example of symbolic expression, in mathematics the sign, + , is used to represent adding one quantity to another.

In each of these examples, separate elements are combined by the relationships given to produce new elements or products.

Many other types of relationships are used to link elements and compounds together within each of these forms.

Relationships are used within each symbolic form as a means of building more complex structures, in order to represent more complex phenomena.

As with associations, relationships inferred between different phenomena are often learned processes, which may or may not truly represent external actualities.

Once these relationships are learned, the individual may continue to see them despite encountering contradictory evidence.

As habitual processes, the relationships can be kept in mind more strongly by the sensory and emotional qualities of the elements and the connections between them.

Further, the associations one has linked to the elements involved in relationships are different for each individual.

This means that two separate individuals can observe the same event occurring, and infer two completely incorrect interpretations.

For example, when two or more individuals observe the scene of an accident, radically different perceptions of the events are often made.

Modern science is a set of principles and procedures designed to minimize perceptual and inferential errors. This is done by establishing a means of testing and retesting the relationships inferred between observable events.

This procedure works best when we maintain a continuously open mind. As soon as we make an assumption about a specific set of phenomena, we begin to focus on and believe the specific set of relationships chosen.

This process creates selective perception, where we begin to see and believe what we expect to see. This limits our range of awareness and understanding.

A more creative and flexible approach is to realize that every formulated thought, association, and relationship is merely an assumption about an external or internal event.

These are attempts to represent to ourselves and to each other what we perceive and believe to be true about what we call reality.

Understanding the world around us and ourselves is greatly facilitated by learning how to rearrange the thoughts we associate together, and the relationships we construct to build more complex structures of thought.

The principles developed in the last section to alter associations can also be applied to change the structure of existing relationships and to create new relationships.

The different types of relationships that can be formulated are as vast as the human imagination.

Some relationships link together simple elements following some rule or principle, and other relationships link together more complex sets of elements.

Learning how to change the nature of the relationships we use to link together different thoughts give us a fundamental key to creative thinking.

One approach to rearranging our thoughts, although cumbersome, has already been given.

The Association Table could be applied to each of the elements or sets of elements within a given relationship, in the hopes of finding new relationships between the given elements.

For example, if A is related to B, we could generate many more associations to A and B which helps modify, define, or otherwise specify the two given elements.

As the new associations are compared and contrasted, giving more complex insights, we will infer more relationships that exist between the two given elements.

As a concrete example of this use of the Association Table, suppose we start with: *fear is the opposite of love.*

By generating associations to the concepts of fear and love, we might also infer that fear is the absence of love; that love helps us surmount fear; and that while love attracts others, fear repels them.

Thus, we can obtain new insights to the given elements in the relationship by comparing and contrasting the associations we formulate to each.

Unfortunately, this application of the Association Table to the generation of creative relationships is sometimes tedious and time-consuming.

Through the course of our daily activities, it is more useful to have a few simple rules of thumb that we can apply at any time to a given situation.

One rule of thumb that is quick and easy to apply to semantic associations is found by comparing and contrasting elements.

It is helpful to think of this approach schematically, using what might be called a *verbal constellation*.

A verbal constellation is created around the two given elements or sets of elements in a relationship, sparking many creative ideas.

To demonstrate this technique, suppose we are given the two elements "fair" and "dark" and told that they are oppositely related (many types of relationships might pertain here).

We can then draw two columns as shown in Figure 1, where one column is named *"Function,"* referring to associations to be drawn that have the same meaning as the given elements.

The second column is labeled *"Form,"* referring to associations that sound similar to the given elements.

Along the function dimension, we list associations that have meanings the same as, or similar to, the given words. Along the form dimension, we list words that have a sound similar to the given words.

This verbal constellation of associations can then be used to generate different types of creative relationships.

Puns are easily created from the constellation by finding word substitutions, that have a sound or meaning similar to either of the given words.

For example, suppose we think of the sentence, *"The socialite's complexion was fair."*

We could then make a pun by saying, *"The socialite's complexion was fare,"* meaning the socialite's appearance paid her admission into societal functions.

Here, the word substitution has a sound similar to the given word.

Figure 1

VERBAL CONSTELLATION

Fair				Dark
Similar Sounds	Similar Meanings		Similar Meanings	Similar Sounds
(Form Dimension) Dimensions)	(Function Dimensions		(Function Dimensions)	(Form

ANTONYMS

Hair Lark	Light	<------>	Shade
Stair Hark	Bright	<------>	Obtuse
Wear Stark	Clear	<------>	Obscure
Fare Park	Honest	<------>	Shadow

EXERCISES

WONDERFUL   TERRIBLE

BEAUTIFUL   UGLY

Observing Figure 1, it is noted that since the two given words are opposite in meaning, the synonyms drawn from the two given words become antonyms. That is, synonyms to "fair" are antonyms to the synonyms of "dark."

If this terminology is confusing, it is hoped Figure 1 will make the point clear. We can then use the two sets of synonyms to make paradoxical titles for books, plays, or stories. Various creativity tests assess our ability to make up creative titles for stories.

Applying the words given in Figure 1 to the invention of paradoxical titles, we could invent the titles, *"The Bright Shadows,"* or *"The Obtuse Light."*

Paradoxes can be powerfully expressive, since they express two opposite concepts at once.

As further practice, do the same with the words given under "Exercises" in Figure 1. Then try to think of other types of creative relationships that can be drawn from this verbal constellation.

Further, what other forms of verbal constellations can you think of that might be helpful to the generation of creative relationships?

Remember that verbal constellations are based on the idea of comparing and contrasting words and the concepts behind them, by looking at the form and function of the words and the associations drawn from them.

In a sense, we are schematically observing different dimensions of the words, to find creative relationships between them.

A similar quick and easy procedure can be applied to figural associations, using what we might call a *spatial constellation.*

A spatial constellation is created by allowing a given figure to vary spatially in every way that we might imagine, so as to stimulate creative ideas.

To demonstrate this technique, suppose that we are given the figure of a brick, and asked to produce as many unusual uses as possible for the brick. Many creativity measures assess unusual uses for common objects.

We can begin by listing the sensory dimensions of a brick, such as length, width, height, color, density, and material composition.

We then list as many unusual uses as we can for the brick as given, as shown in Figure 2.

These uses might include: a doorstop, a counterbalance for a pulley system, an anchor for a canoe, and a headrest for a yogi.

The next step of the procedure is to imagine each of the listed dimensions of the brick to change while holding the other dimensions constant.

We could imagine the length of the brick to vary, from perhaps one inch to a thousand miles, producing very different ideas about it's potential uses.

For example, the tiny bricks might imaginatively be used as part of a child's playthings, and the immensely long bricks might be used to construct a galactic space station.

Figure 2

SPATIAL CONSTELLATION

Figure/Object	Sketch	Unusual Uses
Brick		doorstop, counterbalance, anchor, headrest
Dimensions		
length		child's toys, galactic space station
width		Cosmic stair steps
height		towering planks
color (brown)		multispectral sculptures
density (heavy)		building block in anti-gravity machine; center of gravity in space station
material composition		seawall water filter; part of igloo

Similarly, we could imagine the width and height of the brick to vary, perhaps sparking imaginative thoughts of cosmic stair steps for giants and towering planks for the walls of Troy.

Clearly, the ideas we invent from these procedures might pertain more closely to science fiction than to daily realities, so that the usefulness of any given idea has to be individually assessed with reference to the problem to be solved.

Next, we might imagine the color of the brick to vary, perhaps sparking thoughts of multispectral sculptures composed of many such bricks.

Then, we would imagine the density of the brick to vary, perhaps from a light and airy object to one heavier than the Earth.

The light and airy brick might be used as a building block in an imaginary anti-gravity machine, and the infinitely heavy brick might be used as the center of gravity in constructing a space station to orbit the Earth.

Finally, we would imagine the material composition of the brick to vary, perhaps as a porous substance to one of frozen water.

The porous brick might be used as a part of a seawall to filter water, and the frozen brick might be used as part of an igloo.

Many novel ideas can be generated by using this form of spatial constellation.

Some of the ideas might be germane to the problem or issue under consideration; others will certainly not be useful.

Through the creation of many ideas, however, it becomes more likely that some useful ideas will arise.

It is important to keep an open mind toward any of the formulations that are generated.

Many unexpected discoveries and ideas might be found in addition to, or instead of, the originally intended target solution – serendipity at play.

Remember that spatial constellations are created by allowing a given figure to vary spatially in every way we can imagine.

The success of the constellation in generating novel ideas is in part contingent on how many dimensions or different aspects of the figure we initially identify.

It is helpful to sketch how the figure changes as each of its dimensions is allowed to change, as shown in Figure 2.

Exercise 17.A:

Using Figure One as a guide, create a verbal constellation out of the word pair high-low. Create the constellation in your notebook. Then make as many puns and paradoxical titles as you can from the constellation.

Exercise 17.B:

Using Figure 2 as a guide, create a spatial constellation out of the figure of a pyramid. Write the constellation in your notebook, then allow each of the dimensions of the pyramid to vary while holding the other dimensions constant.

Think of as many uses as you can for each of the resulting figures.

Verbal and spatial constellations, as well as the Association Table, are but a few examples of how creative relationships can be generated. There are as many means of generating such relationships as we can imagine.

The only limit we have upon this process is the limit we decide to impose upon ourselves.

Just as the free and open mind is most receptive to novel ideas, so is the open mind best able to formulate new means or approaches designed to spark even more ideas and relationships.

Here, we are creating new relationships that give birth to still more creative relationships.

Since creative ideas can be born at any time by anybody, it is helpful to allow our mind the flexibility necessary to perceive such ideas.

This is accomplished not only through the relaxed attention and the creative self-perception previously pointed out, but through allowing our mind to constantly shift and vary the relationships that bind thoughts together.

This is best achieved by applying the principle of *co-variation* to every thought we think. This practice is less formidable then it sounds, since once it becomes a habit it is quite easy to do.

The principle of co-variation simply states that we allow a thought to change in terms of its shape, form, function, and motion, while holding the other thoughts associated with it constant.

The Association Table and the verbal and spatial constellations are all examples of the use of the principle of co-variation in specific forms.

Other examples of co-variation are found throughout mathematics, physics, chess, creative writing, drama, and wherever individuals compare the relative effect of changing one element to the effects on other elements in a given set.

Formally, co-variation can be described as the process of observing how changing one variable or dimension of an object affects other variables or other given dimensions of the object under consideration.

The concept of density illustrates well the principle of co-variation. Suppose we know that the density of an object increases as its mass increases, and that the density decreases as the volume of the object increases.

Combining these two concepts together, we can derive that density equals mass divided by volume.

Here, density is said to co-vary with mass and volume, meaning that a change in mass or volume gives a change in density, and the changes follow a ruled relationship.

Similarly, if we perceive a set of variables as maintaining certain fixed relationships to one another, then changing one of the variables will change the others as well.

Applying this process to our thoughts and emotions gives us greater control over our behavior, as described in the text of the Fifth Day.

In fact, this process can be applied to any form of symbolic expression.

As previously explained, semantic and figural means of expression are different forms of a more general symbolic expression performed by humans, where external or internal states are represented by symbols.

Analogously, the principle of co-variation is the more generic means of creatively rearranging our perceptions, just as the Association Table, and the verbal and spatial constellations are specific examples.

Applying the principle of co-variation to the full realm of symbolic expression gives us an important key to the creative mastery of our world.

Using the self-suggestion techniques presented on days 2 and 3 of this text, use your imagination to think of how applying the technique of co-variation in your daily life might benefit you.

Remember:

Relationships link together information from figural, semantic, and symbolic forms, following some rule or constructed principle, often producing a new element or product.

Like associations, relationships can become habitual processes and are affected by the sensory, emotional, and associative properties of the elements and connections involved.

Relationships can link together simple e l e m e n t s   o r   m o r e   c o m p l e x arrangements of elements.

Like associations, relationships can be restructured using the Association Table.

Associations drawn from each of the e l e m e n t s   o r   c o m p o u n d s   i n   t h e r e l a t i o n s h i p   a r e   c o m p a r e d   a n d contrasted, with the hopes of finding new relationships between the separate sets of ideas.

Another means of generating creative relationships for semantic information is found with the verbal constellation, w h e r e   t h e   f u n c t i o n   a n d   f o r m dimensions of the two related words are compared and contrasted in a quest for creative relationships.

A spatial constellation can be used to generate creative ideas for figural information, by allowing the dimensions of the figure to change while holding the other dimensions constant.

These techniques represent but a few of those possible in the generation of creative relationships and ideas, and are specific examples of the principle of co-variation.

This principle can be applied to any form of symbolic thought, since it consists of allowing one thought to change at a time in terms of its shape, form, function, and motion, while holding the other thoughts associated with it constant.

The principle of co-variation is the essence of the creative process, since it allows us to change at will the realities we wish to create.

Before you go to sleep tonight, review these concepts and tell your subconscious mind that you will remember these ideas and that you will attain a deeper and deeper understanding of the concepts and how to apply them in your daily life.

Start thinking now about various ways in which you can apply these ideas to problems you are presently facing or expecting to face in the future.

Make these creativity ideas a part of your mental repertoire, and make a regular habit of observing the patterns of your thinking processes.

You will be rewarded many times over by the insights you obtain to your own thoughts, feelings, and behavior as you piece together the interconnections of mental processes which you might otherwise have taken for granted.

Making these techniques your personal habits will give you a greater sense and degree of control over your life, as you actively direct your mind to function the way you want it to function.

Rather than being controlled by habits you formed years ago, you can change and re-create your personal habits as you choose and as situational circumstances change around you.

As you apply these techniques to your daily affairs and problems, you will discover a new sense of freedom and self-worth, and a greater mastery over your environment.

This is the essence of creativity.

Tomorrow you will have a chance to apply these newly learned techniques to a number of creativity tasks, as you work your way through "Practicing Creativity, Part 2."

SEVENTH DAY

Seventh Day: Practicing Creativity

Part 2

Today gives you a second chance to put your evolving creative abilities to work. What follows are a number of exercises analogous to the ones you completed while taking "Developing Creativity, Part 1."

Although the exercises take the same form, the questions are different.

As with the exercises given on the Fourth Day, the following exercises give you recommended time limits within which to work.

Try to follow these limits because they teach you to think creatively on the spot. Now relax, and allow your thoughts to flow in original patterns.

When you are ready, turn the page and begin.

Practicing Creativity

Part 2

Exercise 18: This is a measure to see how many things you can think of that are alike in some way.

For example, if you were asked to list all the things you can think of that are violet, you might list "*violets – the flower,*" "*twilight,*" and so on.

You may use one word, several words, or a phrase to describe each thing. Allow yourself about *three minutes* to complete this exercise.

The category is "*hollow.*" List all the things you can in your notebook that are hollow.

Exercise 19:   When you are thinking creatively, it is often helpful to think in sequences of images and words that are somehow linked together.

To practice thinking in sequences, this measure requires you to think of words having meanings which are the same as, or similar to, a given word.

For example, if you were given the word long, you might write "*lengthy*," "*extended*," "*tiresome*," and so on. Write down as many words as you can, allowing yourself about *five minutes* to complete the exercise.

In your notebook, for each of the following three words, write as many words as you can that have meanings similar to the given word:

Slow   Strong   Light

Exercise 20: When trying to find creative answers, you can often see things in a new light by rearranging how you categorize certain objects or ideas.

You can practice this type of mental flexibility by listing as many objects as you can which belong to any given class of objects.

In this exercise, your task will be to list as many objects as you can which belong to the given class.

For example, if you were given the class "*dog*," you might list "*terrier*," "*spaniel*," "*collie*," and so on. Allow yourself about *two minutes* to complete this exercise.

In the space below, list as many things as you can that belong to the class "*gases*."

Exercise 21: Creative ideas often come from finding new uses for common objects. In this exercise, you are to list as many uses as you can for the given object.

For example, if you were asked to list all the uses you can for a piece of string, you might include *"picture hanger,"* *"teeth cleaner,"* *"toy hat strap,"* and so on.

Your answers can be realistic or completely imaginary. Allow yourself about *five minutes* to complete this exercise.

In your notebook, list as many uses as you can for a, *"sheet of aluminum foil."*

Exercise 22: Another important aspect of creativity is learning how to express complex ideas in a simple form. One means of practicing this is creating titles for a given story plot.

In this exercise, you will be given a story plot and asked to write as many titles as you can which represent a plot. The titles can be realistic or imaginative, but they must have some clear relationship to the given plot.

For example, if you were given a plot about a convicted felon becoming the President of the United States, you might call it "*From Parolee to President*," or perhaps, "*Jail to the Chief.*"

Allow yourself about *three minutes* to complete this exercise.

In your notebook, write as many titles as you can for the following plot: A dejected actor had fifteen face lifts in a futile attempt to sustain his mediocre career.

Outcast by all the major motion picture studios, he finally landed a job in the only profession that demands more pretense and make-believe than acting — politics.

Exercise 23: Creative thinking often involves the process of abstraction, where we use metaphors, similes, puns, and other constructions to get our ideas across to others.

Many of these verbal constructions compare one thing to another.

In this exercise, you will be given an incomplete sentence and asked to complete the sentence by comparing the first part of the sentence with as many different things as you can.

For example, if you were given the incomplete sentence, *"Want is _____,"* you might complete it with *"Want is the mistress of invention,"* and *"Want is the burden of the poor,"* and so on.

You can complete the given sentence with a single word, a series of words or a phrase, but make sure the answer relates to the first part of the sentence. Allow yourself about *two minutes* to complete this exercise.

In your notebook, complete the following incomplete sentence with as many comparisons as you can: "*Life is* _____."

EIGHTH DAY

Eighth Day

Final Self-Assessment

During the past seven days, you have completed a number of creativity-stimulating tasks.

You have learned to think about yourself in a more creative manner.

You have studied thinking patterns and how to change them, and you have had the opportunity to put your evolving creative abilities to work by practicing creativity tasks.

You have learned many things which you can take with you to apply to your daily life   and the problems which confront you.

It is especially helpful at this point to obtain some idea about how your creative abilities have grown during the last week.

The following three measures are analogous to the ones you took on the first day of the program, so you can compare today's scores to your earlier performance.

The measures today are of exactly the same form, but the actual questions asked are different.

Again, the measures assess how well you use your imagination and your reasoning power. Each measure is self-explanatory and provides you with a suggested time limit for completing the measure.

To score each measure, you simply add up the number of answers you gave within the suggested time limit.

You will then be given a method of comparing these scores to your performance on the first day.

The first measure determines your ability to make up ideas at will, which describe a given phrase or expression.

The goal is to think of as many things as you can within the given time limit, by letting your imagination play.

The second measure determines your ability to think of as many associations as you can which fit a given category.

As you progress through the measure, the categories of association become more and more complex, challenging you to really concentrate.

As with the first measure, the goal is to think of as many things as you can within the given time limit.

The third measure assesses your ability to think in terms of relationships. You will be asked to think of answers that have different types of relationships to the given words.

As with other measures, the goal is to think of as many answers as you can within the given time limit.

As you work your way through the measures, try to apply everything you have learned from the creativity program.

Repeat your positive self-statements as you approach each task, and apply the creative thinking patterns you have learned.

Remember how you focused your developing abilities upon the practice of creativity tasks, and how you puzzled out the problems.

Reflect for a moment on any original creative thinking patterns that you have discovered, and try to apply them today.

Relax, and enjoy the feeling of accomplishment you have. The familiarity and ease you have in handling these tasks will keep growing and expand in many new directions.

When you are ready, please proceed to the next page and begin.

Measure 4

In this measure, you will be asked to think of as many words or phrases you can which describe the given phrase.

For example, if you were asked to respond to the expression, "*The man was as tall as_____ .*"

You might answer with many different words and phrases. Some of these might be, "*the trees,*" "*the sky,*" "*Wilt Chamberlain,*" and so on.

Your goal is to think of as many answers to the given phrase as you can.

Your score on this measure will be the number of words and phrases you write down which somehow describe the given phrase.

It is important to time yourself on this measure. This final score will be compared to your beginning score on Measure 1, given on the first day of the program.

Allow yourself exactly *five minutes* to complete this measure.

In your notebook, write as many words and phrases as you can think of which complete the given phrases below:

The touch of her hand was like:

The stars looked like:

The taste of the water was as sweet as:

The spring flowers smelled like:

After you have completed Measure 4 within the five-minute time limit, simply add up the number of separate words and phrases you wrote down for all four parts of the measure combined.

Write your total score in your notebook as follows:

Measure 4 Total Score:

Measure 5

In this measure, you will be given certain words or combinations of words, and your task will be to list as many associations to the words as you can.

For example, if you were asked, "Name everything you can that is orange," you might answer with "*the sun*," "a *beach umbrella*," "*oranges from Florida*," and so on.

As with the previous measure, your goal is to think of as many answers to the given words as you can.

Your score on this measure will be the number of things you write down which fit the category described by the given words.

It is also important to time yourself on this measure, so this final score can be compared fairly to your beginning score on Measure 2, given the first day of the program.

Allow yourself exactly *two minutes* to complete each of the three parts of this measure.

When you are ready, turn to the next page and begin.

In your notebook, write down as many things as you can think of which fit the given categories below:

Name everything you can that is red:

Name everything you can that is red and hot:

Name everything you can that is red, hot and young:

After you have completed Measure 5 within the *six-minute* total time limit, simply add up the number of separate things you wrote down for all three parts of the measure combined.

Write your total score in your notebook as follows:

Measure 5 Total Score:

Measure 6

In this measure, you will be given a certain word, and your task will be to think of as many answers as you can that have different specific relationships to the given word.

You will be asked to think of synonyms, antonyms, and words that rhyme with the given word.

For example, if you were given the word *tight*, you would be asked to list as many words as you can that rhyme with tight.

Next, list as many words as you can that have the same meaning as tight.

Then, as many words as you can that have a meaning opposite to tight.

Your score on this measure will be the number of answers you write down which properly relate to the given word.

As with the previous two measures, it is important to time yourself so your score can be compared to Measure 3, given on the first day of the program.

Allow yourself exactly *two minutes* to complete each of the three parts of this measure. When you are ready, proceed to the next page and begin.

The given word is "*light*," as in "*not heavy*."

In your notebook, write down as many words as you can that rhyme with or sound like light:

Next, write as many words as you can that have the same or similar meaning to the word light:

Finally, write as many words as you can that have the opposite or nearly opposite meaning to the word light:

After you have completed Measure 6 within the six-minute total time limit, simply add up the number of separate things you wrote down for all three parts of the measure combined.

Write your total score in your notebook as follows:

Measure 6 Total Score:

Calculating Your Creativity Quotient

Now that you have completed a number of measures before and after taking the creativity program, it is possible to calculate your percentage of improvement on the measures given.

Using these percentages, we will calculate your Creativity Quotient.

This quotient is not analogous to an intelligence quotient, nor is it normed or standardized against a sample population.

It is simply a proportion telling you how much your creative ability has increased relative to the measures given.

It is important to realize that your creative potential might have grown in ways which measures do not assess.

In the same way that intelligence quotients are biased toward one's academic orientation and performance, this creativity quotient is biased toward one's innate or learned ability to perform well on these types of measures.

Therefore, the most important thing for you to look for is the amount you have improved on these tasks.

This can serve as a diagnostic measure for you, pointing out the areas of creative performance you might want to work on in the future.

For example, if your scores increase significantly on Ratios A and B below, but not on C, then this indicates your use of free-flowing imagination has appreciably increased, but your use of reasoning may not have.

You might then review days five and six of the program, covering the development of creative thinking patterns.

Conversely, if your performance should increase on Ratio C, but not on A and B, then you might review days two and three as well as days four and six, to help those imaginative ideas flow.

Ratio D is an average of all the other three ratios, giving you an overall assessment of your improvement on these creativity tasks.

If this ratio should not register an increase in your performance, then you might want to review the entire creativity program.

Do not be discouraged if your scores do not increase greatly, or if they even decrease.

It may well be that ideas are busily sinking into your mind at deeper levels, and it will take time before the concepts produce a change in your behavior.

For each of the three self-assessment measures, your score obtained after taking the creativity program will be put in the numerator of the ratio.

Your score obtained before taking the program will be put in the denominator.

This figure is then multiplied by 100 to give your creativity ratios. This means that a score above 100 means an increase in performance, and a score below 100 means a decrease.

Finally, Ratio D is calculated, which is an average of the other three ratios. Ratio D gives your Creativity Quotient for the three self-assessment measures.

To calculate your creativity ratios and your Creativity Quotient, write down the scores in your notebook you obtained on Measures 1 through 6 as indicated.

Ratio A: Fill in your notebook the scores you obtained on Measures 1 and 4. Then calculate the ratio:

$$\text{Ratio A} = \frac{\text{Measure 4}}{\text{Measure 1}} \times 100 = \underline{\qquad}.$$

Ratio B: Fill in your notebook the scores you obtained on Measures 2 and 5. Then calculate the ratio:

$$\text{Ratio B} = \frac{\text{Measure 5}}{\text{Measure 2}} \times 100 = \underline{\qquad}.$$

Ratio C: Fill in your notebook the scores you obtained on Measures 3 and 6. Then calculate the ratio:

Ratio C = $\dfrac{\text{Measure 6}}{\text{Measure 3}}$ X 100 = .

Ratio D: Fill in your notebook the scores you calculated for Ratios A, B, C. Then calculate Ratio D:

Ratio D = $\dfrac{\text{Ratio A + Ratio B + Ratio C}}{3}$ =

Ratio D: Is your overall Creativity Quotient.

CONGRATULATIONS !

CONCLUSION

The entire purpose of this creativity program has been to stimulate your creative abilities along a number of different dimensions, with the hope that you will take these ideas and apply them to your daily life.

They can be used in daily problem solving, in relating more flexibly to other people, and in seeing ourselves in a more positive light.

You have been shown how to perceive yourself differently, taking the habits and perceptions of your present self-concept and learning how to mold and restructure them into a new **YOU**.

These are principles you might want to share with others, to help them adopt a more creative and flexible attitude toward life as well.

Remember to repeat your positive self-statements whenever you need or desire, replacing any negative self-statements that might arise.

Determine to use your subconscious mind on a daily basis, feeding it suggestions and then allowing it to go to work.

You have learned how thinking patterns form, and how you can readily change them.

Realizing that many of our habits of thought and behavior are the product of random experiences, we obtain a new sense of power and control over our lives by learning how to change those habits at will.

Remember to use the principles built into the Association Table, the verbal and spatial constellations, and the principle of co-variation in restructuring your thoughts, feelings, and behavior.

As with the use of positive self-statements, these techniques require time and patience for you to obtain the maximum benefit from them.

Make a habit to review these ideas often, and try to invent your own techniques for stimulating creative ideas.

Make up your own patterns of thinking, constantly searching for better ways of understanding the world around you.

Use the positive self-statements and your subconscious as you evolve your original thinking patterns.

Finally, you have been allowed to practice a range of creativity tasks to help you focus on applying these techniques to your daily world.

Remember to apply the positive self-statements and the creative thinking patterns to problems you encounter, and to share these concepts with others.

Find ways to make these concepts work for you, allowing your mind to become and remain flexible.

Decide now to create your own world as much as possible, rather than passively being controlled by circumstances or other people around you.

Decide now to make creativity a part of your life.

The quality of life for all humankind depends upon the creative power we collectively wield, and upon our creatively restructuring the illusions and confused emotions which have long dominated the human race.

REFERENCES

Barron, F., & Harrington, D.M. (1981). Creativity, intelligence, and personality. Annual Review of Psychology, 32, 439-476.

Blanchard, K., & Johnson, S. (1982). The One Minute Manager. New York: Berkley Books.

Busse, T.V., & Mansfield, R.S. (1980). Theories of the creative process: A review and a perspective. Journal of Creative Behavior, 14(2), 91-103; 132.

Carnegie, D. (1981). How to Win Friends and Influence People (rev. ed.). New York: Pocket Books.

Cialdini, R. (2016). Pre-Suasion. New York: Simon & Shuster.

Clymer, R.S. (1945). The Interpretation of St. Matthew. Vol. I, II. Quakertown, PA: Beverly Hall Corporation.

Cohen, L.W., & Ehrlich, G. (1963). The Structure of the Real Number System. Princeton, NJ: D. Van Nostrand Co., Inc.

Corsini, R.J. & Contributors. (1979). Current Psychotherapies. Itasca, IL: F.E. Peacock Publishers, Inc.

Dalrymple, R. (2016). I Love You, God. N. Ft. Myers, FL: Celestial Gifts Publishing.

Dalrymple, R. (2015). Paradise Found 2015 (Film). N. Ft. Myers, FL: Dalrymple Brothers Films.

Dalrymple, R. (2016). Quantum Field Psychology. N. Ft. Myers FL: Celestial Gifts Publishing.

Dalrymple, R. (2016). The Inner Manager. N. Ft. Myers, FL: Celestial Gifts Publishing.

DeBono, E. (1967). The Five Day Course in Thinking. New York: Basic Books.

Dumas, Alexandre. (1990). The Three Musketeers. New York: Baronet Books. (Original work published 1844).

Einstein, A. (1961). Relativity: The Special and the General Theory (R. Lawson, Trans.). New York: Bonanza Books.

Erickson, M.H. (1969). A special inquiry with Aldous Huxley into the nature and character of various states of consciousness. In C.T. Tart (Ed.), Altered States of Consciousness. New York: Wiley.

Frank, J.D. (1974). Persuasion and Healing. New York: Schocken Books.

Freud, S. (1952). On Dreams (James Strachey, Trans.). New York: W.W. Norton & Company, Inc. (Original work published 1901).

Freud, S. (1958). On Creativity and the Unconscious. New York: Harper & Row. (Original work published 1925).

Freud, S. (1960). The Psychopathology of Everyday Life (Alan Tyson, Trans.). New York: W.W. Norton & Company, Inc. (Original work published 1901).

Gendlin, E. (1969). Focusing. Psychotherapy: Theory, Research and Practice, 6, 4-15.

Glover, J.A. (1977). Risky shift and creativity. Social Behavior and Personality, 5(2), 317-320.

Gordon, W.J.J. (1961). Synectics. New York: Harper.

Greenson, R.R. (1967). The Technique and Practice of Psychoanalysis (Vol. 1). New York: International Universities Press, Inc.

Guilford, J.P. (1957). Creative abilities in the arts. Psychological Review, 64, 110-118.

Hadramard, J. (1945). The Psychology of Invention in the Mathematical Field. Princeton: Princeton University Press.

Hill, Napoleon. (1988). Think and Grow Rich. New York: Fawcett Columbine.

Holtje, Dennis. (1995). From Light to Sound. Albuquerque, NM: MasterPath, Inc.

Holy Bible. (1977). New Revised Standard Version . New York: Oxford University Press.

Hummel, J.A. (1967). Introduction to Vector Functions. Reading, MA: Addison-Wesley.

Jones, E. (1953). The Life and Work of Sigmund Freud. (Vol. 1). New York: Basic Books.

Fillmore, Charles. (1930). The Twelve Powers of Man. Unity Village, MO: Unity Books.

Fillmore, Charles. (1953). Keep a True Lent. Unity Village, MO: Unity Books.

Fillmore, Charles. (1949). Atom-Smashing Power of Mind. Unity Village: Unity Books.

Fillmore, Charles. (1936). Prosperity. Unity Village, MO: Unity Books.

Foster, Jean K. (1994). The Truth That Goes Unclaimed. Warrensburg, MO: Team Up.

Foster, Jean K. (1987). The God-Mind Connection. Warrensburg, MO: Team Up.

Jung, C.G. (1974). Dreams (R.F.C. Hull, Trans.).

Princeton, NJ: Princeton University Press. Kubie, L.S. (1958). Neurotic distortions of the creative process. Lawrence, KS: U. of Kansas Press.

Kuhn, T.S. (1970). The structure of scientific revolutions (2nd ed.), 2(2). Chicago: The University of Chicago.

Lorayne, H. (1985). Page-A-Minute Memory Book. New York: Holt, Rinehart and Winston.

Mandino, O. (1968). The Greatest Salesman in the World. New York: Bantam Books.

Maslow, K. (1959). Creativity in self-actualizing people. In H. Anderson (Ed.), Creativity and Its Cultivation. New York: Harper.

Meichenbaum, D. (1975). Enhancing creativity by modifying what subjects say to themselves. American Educational Research Journal, 12(2), 129-145.

Moise, E. (1967). Calculus. Reading, MA: Addison-Wesley Publishing Company.

Mueller, L.K. (1978). Beneficial and detrimental modeling effects on creative response production. The Journal of Psychology, 98, 253-260.

Osborn, A.F. (1963). Applied Imagination (3rd ed.). New York: Scribner & Sons.

Ouspensky, P.D. (1982). Tertium Organum. (E. Kadloubovsky, Trans.). New York: Vintage Books. (Original work published 1922).

Parnes, S.J. (1967). Creative Behavior Guidebook. New York: Scribner & Sons.

Patterson, C.H. (1986). Theories of Counseling and Psychotherapy (4th ed.). New York: Harper & Row.

Ponder, Catherine. (1987). The Dynamic Laws of Prayer.

Marina del Ray, CA: DeVorss & Company.

Ponder, Catherine. (1967). The Healing Secrets of the Ages.
Marina del Ray, CA: DeVorss & Company.

Ponder, Catherine. (1966). The Dynamic Laws of Healing.
Marina del Ray, CA: DeVorss & Company.

Ponder, Catherine. (1966). The Prospering Power of Love. Marina del Ray, CA: DeVorss & Company.

Powell, J. (1974). The Secret of Staying in Love. Allen, TX: Argus Communications.

Prince, G.M. (1970). The Practice of Creativity. New York: Harper.

Rimm, D.C., & Masters, J.C. (1979). Behavior Therapy: Techniques and Empirical Findings (2nd ed.). New York: Academic Press.

Robinson, D. (1981). An Intellectual History of Psychology. New York: Macmillan.

Sims, B.T. (1976). Fundamentals of Topology. New York: Macmillan.

Spalding, Baird T. (1924, 1937, 1964). Life and Teaching
of the Masters of the Far East (Vol. I). Marina del Rey, CA: DeVorss Publications.

Spalding, Baird T. (1927, 1937, 1944, 1972). Life and Teaching of the Masters of the Far East (Vol. II). Marina del Rey, CA: DeVorss Publications.

Spalding, Baird T. (1935). Life and Teaching of the Masters of the Far East (Vol. III). Marina del Rey, CA: DeVorss Publications.

Spalding, Baird T. (1948). Life and Teaching of the Masters of the Far East (Vol. IV). Marina del Rey, CA: DeVorss Publications.

Spalding, Baird T. (1955). Life and Teaching of the Masters of the Far East (Vol. V). Marina del Rey, CA: DeVorss Publications.

Spalding, Baird T. (1996). Life and Teaching of the Masters of the Far East (Vol. VI). Marina del Rey, CA: devours Publications.

Stein, M.I. (1974). Stimulating Creativity (Vol. 1). New York: Academic Press.

Stein, M.I. (1975). Stimulating Creativity (Vol. 2). New York: Academic Press.

Torrance, E.P. (1962). Guiding Creative Talent. Englewood Cliffs, NJ: Prentice-Hall.

Vick, J.W. (1973). Homology Theory: An Introduction to Algebraic Topology. San Diego, CA: Academic Press.

Walkup, L.E. (1965). Creativity in science through visualization. Perceptual and Motor Skills, 21, 35-41.

Wallas, G. (1926). The Art of Thought. New York: Harcourt.

Wiener, N. (1961). Cybernetics: or Control and Communication in the Animal and the Machine (2nd ed.). Cambridge, MA: The M.I.T. Press.

Yogananda, Paramahansa. (1982). Man's Eternal Quest.
Los Angeles, CA: Self-Realization Fellowship.

OTHER BOOKS BY DR. RON DALRYMPLE:

THE INNER MANAGER
Mastering Business, Home and Self
by Dr. Ron Dalrymple

"Profound, the guidebook of a lifetime."
----- The Book Reader

"Imaginative...well-written...plausible."
----- West Coast Review of Books

"Thank-you for sending me this wonderful book."
—- Louise Hay, Best-Selling Author

Seeking a better life for himself and his family, a young man meets a woman executive who takes him on a fascinating journey to his inner mind.

He discovers a wealth of talents and powers long hidden beneath his fears and doubts.

In a step-by-step process, he learns he can activate his energy and resources to take a Quantum Leap to a higher level of self-creative thought, offering him virtually unlimited success in life...but it is up to him to make it happen.

He learns how to use the living software of his thoughts to reprogram the hardware of his brain and nervous system, shifting his conscious state and available energy at will.

He discovers the true powers of thought, concentration, will-power, visualization, desire, memory, deductive and inductive reasoning, the infinitizing power of pure love and much more.

He begins to absorb and understand the simple but integrative concepts of Quantum Field Psychology, unveiling the keys to creating a successful life and building a dynamic business.

He learns that by creating his own business or by creating his own niche in his current place of employment, he can take responsibility for his life at a whole new level and truly become the master of his own destiny.

The young man discovers his own Inner Manager, the executive power within his being always waiting to be called to duty.

QUANTUM FIELD PSYCHOLOGY
The Thoton Particle Theory
by Dr. Ron Dalrymple

Dr. Ron Dalrymple, a licensed psychologist in multiple states, has developed an integration of modern-day psychologies with Einsteinian physics and topological mathematics known as Quantum Field Psychology.

Quantum Field Psychology starts with the premise that the mind is more than the mere result of the interactions of biochemicals and matter found within the brain, as reductionists and Cartesian thinkers insist.

Dr. Dalrymple works from the theoretical basis that the mind is an energy field that subfuses but transcends the physical brain. His first premise is that thought energy propagates through space in a wave form, but interacts with matter as a particle.

The smallest unit, or quantum of thought is the thoton (Dalrymple, 1978), just as the photon is the quantum of light.

The second premise of Quantum Field Psychology is that every thought is a form of living software that programs the Superconscious Mind to function in specific ways.

This affects not only the hardware of the brain and nervous system, but the external world of the individual as well.

This suggests the awesome power of thought when properly trained, focused and concentrated on specific results, especially when powered by intense emotional energy over a period of time.

The third premise of Quantum Field Psychology is that the power of thought can seed an entire universe, and that the first step toward greater mental and planetary health and success in life is to transform all of one's negative thoughts and feelings into positive ones.

Although this sounds elementary, it is most difficult to do.

Try having only positive thoughts and feelings for a month, instantly re-creating all negative thoughts and feelings as soon as they arise.

The fourth premise is that by re-integrating and re-creating one's mind and personality with the techniques of Quantum Field Psychology, the individual can make a series of quantum leaps into universes once beyond her or his imagination.

Dr. Dalrymple's works develop, illustrate and expand upon these premises in simple terms.

This helps the reader better understand his or her innate human potential in order to master life and become the greatest success one can be.

Dr. Dalrymple offers seminars to corporate, university, professional and multi-level marketing groups on a diversity of topics.

These areas include success/motivation, systems analysis, creativity and tapping the power of the Superconscious Mind.

I LOVE YOU, GOD

Proverbs of Peace, Prosperity and Power for the Third Millennium

by Dr. Ron Dalrymple

The purpose of this book is to help the reader focus on Divine ideas every day.

Since what we dwell upon comes upon us, it is important to make a habit of thinking positive, healthy, Divine, inspirational, loving thoughts all day, no matter what other people are doing around us or to us.

One of the greatest difficulties in transforming oneself to a more Divine attitude and perspective is found in working through the negative emotions and beliefs we have long internalized.

These beliefs and emotions become lodged in the subconscious mind, and drive the system automatically until they are changed.

This takes considerable effort and persistence, since the deeply embedded negative emotions tend to link to many different thoughts, attitudes and other feelings.

A virtual labyrinth of interconnected thoughts, emotions and behaviors have to be transformed.

This book was created to help the reader achieve that goal.

The intent is for the reader to dwell upon each affirmation of the day with strong feeling, trying to love the very idea being expressed, and projecting it outward to the world.

Each affirmation should be repeated many times throughout the day, and memorized for future use. As you practice these, your own affirmations will occur to you. Use them all with devotion, because what you worship, is what you become.

PARADISE FOUND 2015
A Film Written, Directed and Produced
by
Dr. Ron Dalrymple

An 18-year-old   NASA scientist
discovers a new theory of mind that can
change the world, and has spent his life
in exile proving the theory.

Traveling the world to discover the
hidden secrets of mind.

Laboring through graduate school to
understand where most psychological
systems have failed.

Suppressed and sabotaged by the
tyrannical dinosaurs of academic and
professional delusion, he finally
completes his shocking new theory,
Quantum Field Psychology.

He confronts his dying father, a dictatorial CIA agent and World War II veteran experiencing PTSD with flashbacks to combat, sex-capades in Paris and surreal visions.

The story comes to an explosive conclusion, as the old man arrives at a shocking realization...too late.

Starring Daniel Dasent, Destiny Thomas and James Robert Wood.

A best-selling film on Amazon.com. www.imdbpro.com.

Email: drrondal@hotmail.com, or write P.O. Box 4466, N. Ft. Myers, Florida 33918. USA.

CELESTIAL GIFTS PUBLISHING
P.O. Box 4466
N. Ft. Myers, Florida 33918 USA

Made in the USA
Las Vegas, NV
02 April 2021

20636882R00134